BRAND
NEW
WORLD

BRAND
NEW
WORLD

Define the Role of Your Brand
to Create a Bold Future

SARAH J. KAY

DEDICATION

To the people and the planet of the future.

Author contact: createaboldfuture@icloud.com

Cover and interior design by Andy Meaden / meadencreative.com

ISBN 978-1-7372-4690-9 (Paperback)

ISBN 978-1-7372-4691-6 (Kindle)

ISBN 978-1-7372-4692-3 (ePub)

CONTENTS

ABOUT THIS BOOK

Brand New World equips next-generation CEOs and CMOs to embrace creative thinking, feel confident in making impactful billion-dollar choices, and harness the power of their brand and leadership teams to create a bold future.

Humanity faces complex global challenges. People around the world want to make progress towards a better life, community, and world and they expect brands to play a role in creating this bold future. **Brand New World** is a clarion call to recognise that it's no longer enough for leaders of powerful brands to be motivated only by financial growth.

The biggest brands have the resources to bring people with shared vision and values together and to mobilise change through their voice on a scale large enough to make a difference. CEOs and CMOs hold the keys to creating a better world but they face significant barriers to leveraging the power of brands to supercharge humanity's progress.

In **Brand New World** you will learn how to:

- Develop a brand vision and strategy which articulates the brand's role in creating a bold future.

- Align resources to create measurable value for all stakeholders beyond financial growth.

- Encourage the next generation of leaders to make choices about how they lead your brand.

ACKNOWLEDGEMENTS

The content of this book was developed over ten years through thousands of coaching conversations, listening to consumers around the world, individual executive interviews, generous expert guidance, and dedicated friends. It burst into life in a metaphorical heartbeat because of your collective wisdom, which is woven throughout the pages of this book. I'm deeply indebted to *all* of you.

Holly Lorincz, your gift of courageous truth was vital in the early days of creating this book. Ron Renard, Cathy Presland, and Kate Dixon, thank you for getting me started and for generously sharing your wisdom and expertise as published authors, and for cheering me on as coaches.

To my co-writer, Rachel Henke, at Become A Published Author Services, **www.becomeapublishedauthor.co.uk**, thank you so very much for patiently and efficiently guiding me through the process of writing and launching this book, and for sharing your creativity and ideas for the future. I absolutely couldn't have done this without you.

To Helen Fletcher, Lynsey Lambert, Chloe Speed, Kathy Gomez, Seana Hannah, Pierre-Laurent Baudey, Lisa Hunefeld and Melissa Capone – thank you sincerely for your unwavering belief in me, for your friendship and guidance, and for spending time with me talking about creating a bold future. Missy, I still can't thank you enough for saving my life. This book would not be here if you hadn't!

Additionally, thank you to Jackie Mathys, William Glenn, Brian Stranko, Aurelia Figueroa, John Dana Chisholm, and Lisa MacCallum for so liberally and kindly sharing your expertise and advice.

Extra special and massive thanks go to Melanie Strong, Tamika Abaka-Wood, and Sion Portman for our shared professional experiences over the past ten years, and for your open-hearted contributions to this book. Your experience and philosophy as brand, innovation, and business leaders make our collective vision for the future tangible and real.

Taking a chance on someone can change the trajectory of their life, so to Edgar Jorrison, Paolo Tubito, Steve Tsoi, Andrew Kilshaw, Davide Grasso, Tom Clark, Mike Yonker, Elizabeth Brouwer, and Mark Parker, I am more grateful to you than you will ever know for giving me the opportunity of a lifetime at Nike. I am a far better human because of each of you. Thank you for helping me to get out of my own way and for encouraging me to follow my heart, make the right choices and do this work.

Thank you, Mark Smith, for your creative direction and for generously supporting the Bodecker Foundation: **www. bodeckerfoundation.org**.

Thank you to Andy Meaden for your beautiful creative **www.meadencreative.com**, and to Yasmin Yarwood for your meticulous eye **www.meticulousproofreading.co.uk**.

Huge thanks to my socially distanced coffee, cocktails, and dog walking crew for your energy and enthusiasm for this project, for asking inspired questions, for listening to me give voice to this project, and for your dedication to meeting outdoors despite the freezing cold and rainy Portland winter. Your curiosity and commitment made this book real in my imagination long before it was physically created.

To Sonic, thank you for keeping me company every single day while I'm writing. And above all to my husband, Steve, thank you for adventuring through life with me, for your support always, but especially in the past six months. The best is yet to come.

CHAPTER 1

VOICE

WHY THIS BOOK?

If anything was possible, what kind of future would you want to create for yourself and for those around you?

Humanity faces complex challenges, and brands and brand leaders can play a huge role in creating a bold future.

Many popular leadership books were written for a pre-2020s context, when the most important boxes for a leader to tick were: drive growth, make a profit, increase the share price, develop better leadership skills, and climb the corporate ladder.

Not only has the macro global context changed dramatically, now roughly sixty-three per cent of the world's population is under the age of forty (that's five billion Gen Z and millennials) and they demand more from us, much more. Their elevated expectations include that the future we build must work for everyone. When properly harnessed, our eco-system of brands has the power to play a major role in creating a bright, bold future for humanity and the planet.

This pivotal moment calls not only for deep reflection on who we are being, but also the need to cultivate a *creative mindset*.

Self-aware leaders already possess a highly developed sense of personal leadership: clarity on who they are being, their point of view, and the impact they want to have on the world. Their business management skills are sophisticated because they understand people are human beings first and perform at their best when they believe in a vision.

This book is not about sharing case studies of what's gone before; there are already plenty of those books. This is about *you* as a leader, and how to infuse energy and originality into solving the world's most pressing problems with the power of your brand.

It's about leaving the old formulas behind and seeing our changing world with fresh eyes.

We face a great deal of disruption, much of it created by us, whether consciously or not. The good news is we have an opportunity to re-think the way we do things and to create a new operating system so we don't continue to destroy each other and the planet.

I believe we have an obligation to turn up the heat on this effort *immediately* so that future generations not only have a chance to survive but also to flourish.

This book is a clarion call to recognise that it's no longer enough for people to be motivated only by their self-interest. It's time to take a step back and look at what we are busy creating; to keep what works and to ditch what doesn't.

Through my experience, and from hundreds of interviews with CEOs, brand, and innovation leaders for this book, it's clear that the difficult reality of managing the day-to-day business, means leaders simply don't get the time and space to think deeply about the role they play, and the role the brand they work for plays in creating the future.

Over the years, I have been surprised to hear people grumble when invited to attend a course that would allow them the time and space to step away from the daily grind, to consider their long-term life or brand strategy. It has always been one of my favourite activities.

With the benefit of hindsight, executives have expressed how they wish they had taken the time out in their thirties and forties to develop a deeper understanding of their gifts and how to make the most of them. They craved connection with what they believed in, a vision of what they wanted their own future to look like, and an understanding and appreciation of the power of their position and voice.

Knowing what they know now, they wish they'd found better alignment between themselves and the company or brand they worked for so they could direct the considerable resources they held in the palm of their hands towards creating a better world.

When you work for a world-class brand with a powerful personality, it's natural to absorb a deep sense of the brand and to embody its values and philosophy. You become an extension of the brand and if you're not careful, the brand identity overpowers your perspective of the world to the degree that you ignore the importance of developing your personal brand, values, and philosophy.

As a certified coach, many people across a spectrum of seniority and disciplines have reached out to me over the years for *coffee*. I stopped logging the coaching hours once I hit two thousand! During those conversations, I learned that most people hold a burning desire to feel fulfilled by their work, valued by their organisation, and to use their creative intelligence to solve problems.

They are hungry to find and create meaning in their lives through their career by connecting their work to their values and philosophy. On all levels, they yearn to make an impact on the journey towards a better life, community, and world.

This book is my way of helping you to do that because your voice matters.

WHY ME?

At age sixteen, I wrote a list of brands I dreamed of working for, and Nike was at the top of my list. It was a bold dream, given my humble start as the daughter of an alcoholic and the adverse childhood experiences that came with it, but through a twist of fate I landed my first job at Reebok UK.

This was especially poignant as the brand was founded in my hometown, Bury, Lancashire, where my grandma had sewn Reebok Classics in a shoe factory. I met my future husband at Reebok, and later, after many years working for global brands in different countries, we relocated to the Netherlands, where I joined the brand of my dreams, Nike, in 2008.

During my first performance review, I remember thinking: *Wait! You're asking me to take responsibility for the Nike brand, and to take the consumer somewhere new?* In those early days, I wasn't sure I was *good enough* to do that.

By the end of 2011, I had certified as a coach (CPCC) and articulated my philosophy for how I wanted to approach my life and career, and I called it *Create a Bold Future*. This philosophy gave a name to how I'd lived my life so far and informed everything I did from that point on, from my approach to my career, to my attitude towards solving problems, to my communication style, to my leadership philosophy, and to how I showed up.

Create a Bold Future is my way of expressing my belief that anything is possible. We are only limited by the audacity of our vision, creativity, and commitment. We can get stuck in challenging places, sometimes for many years, and it ultimately destroys us if we stay there.

Create a Bold Future is my way of showing we don't have to stay in a mindset or circumstance that doesn't work for us. It's a way of saying that you can challenge the status quo. You can see the same situation from a fresh perspective and choose to do things differently. You can create a new vision and develop a strategy, and take bold action to reach your destination.

In 2013, I knew I was fully equipped to leverage the power of brands to create a bold future and I was ready to share it with the world. My years at Nike were a pivotal learning experience in my life and taught me that my voice mattered and made a difference. Through a combination of global business and brand acumen, diverse cultural experiences, the ability to create something out of nothing, and delivering results through coaching, I felt ready to help others to see that their voices matter too.

I worked for Nike for just over twelve years, spanning a variety of locations and roles from Category Brand Director to Head of Global Brand Innovation. After all of this time with Nike, I had developed a deep understanding of the role that a well-positioned global brand plays in people's lives.

WHY YOU?

Humans have historically created solutions that solve problems and ultimately enable humanity to progress. The intention behind the things we build is that they work for us. Technology is a great example: humans created technology to help humanity. Social systems are another example: humans created social systems so that the system could speed up progress. But sometimes, we lose sight of why we created the system in the first place. We give it too much power and it spawns beliefs and behaviours that we don't value or that aren't helpful in our evolution. We behave as though we now serve the system or the technology, instead of the other way around.

Brands can be a super example of this power imbalance in action. Humans create brands to be the face of an innovation that solves a problem and allows humanity to make progress. Over time, some brands have become so powerful that it feels like people no longer work to solve problems, but only to enable the business to profit, sometimes at a significant cost to humanity.

As a leader of a powerful brand, are you clear why your brand exists? Are you clear on the role your brand plays in creating a bold future for humanity? Or has the brand become a slave to the economic system and taken your soul with it?

This is important for you to clarify because, as a leader, you hold the keys to creating a better world. As a collective of corporate and brand leaders, you are responsible for trillions of dollars of resources that could be reinvested and put to work for the benefit of humanity.

Your brand was built to be influential. Whether it's the face of one of the biggest consumer goods, energy, transportation, or technology companies in the world, your brand stands for something. Your brand started out, and hopefully still exists, to solve significant problems.

In becoming one of the biggest brands in the world, did you lose sight of the original intention behind why the brand was created? Did you lose the spirit of boldness, and your sense of purpose and agility? Did you begin to focus more on running the business than serving the consumer?

I've interviewed hundreds of people who identify as Gen Z and millennials around the world, and many expressed the belief that as brands become more powerful, they typically become more self-interested.

Gen Z and millennials infer that brands have been abusing their values for years, by not making meaningful moves towards becoming who they say they are. While there is an awakening at the corporate leadership level that the next decade represents an opportunity to create impact, too many leaders still don't deliver on the grand promises, gestures, and statements made.

Brands are expected to help create a new reality, to break down barriers to progress, and to reinvest some of their profit into the communities that made them successful. People are openly calling for brands to help create a better world, but they don't want brands to have an *us and them* mindset. People want brands to adopt a human approach, to value their relationship with their consumers, and to operate as a partner with trust and transparency. Gen Z and millennials see brands as having the potential of being *one of us*, but only when they take authentic steps to face the challenges of creating a new reality, together.

Creating a new reality starts with leaders embracing a new mindset – a mindset which is open, curious, creative, visionary, imaginative, purposeful, and ethical: a creative mindset. Leaders who understand that elevating and empowering those around them through skills such as listening and coaching can create a better world, faster.

Your voice as a leader and as a human being matters because you are closest to your consumer and the world around them, and the role of your brand in serving them. Your voice and that of your brand are amongst the most powerful tools that exist today to create a bold future.

WHY NOW?

For fifty years, capitalism has ruled our land. Brands have driven growth beyond their creators' wildest dreams, generating immense profit for shareholders, but this model has gone some way to destroying our social fabric and planet. Financial growth is important; without it, we don't have the economic resources to reinvest to make progress. But the critical question is: what is the cost of this growth?

Today, there are many CEOs (Chief Executive Officers) and CMOs (Chief Marketing Officers) of global brands who wield more influence over the future than they realise, and with this immense power comes a responsibility to humanity and the planet.

As we cross the boundary of an imaginary firewall and head into our offices each day, we can no longer afford the lazy luxury of ignoring global challenges and human values just to get the job done.

Why? Because people tell us that our brands will become irrelevant if we don't address the impact they have on issues such as climate change and equality.

Triggered by multiple global disruptions in 2020, the goalposts have shifted; the context and expectations of society have changed. Humanity is now at a crossroads.

Are capitalist brands the cause, or can they become the solution to the problems that humanity, and the planet, face?

Next-generation brand leaders hold the keys to creating a bold future, and so they must be equipped to consider how to channel the powerful force of their brands, both for the health of the business and for the world.

I envision this book as the starting point of an ongoing, open-source conversation between brand leaders.

Let's begin!

COACHING QUESTIONS

Your voice and that of your brand are amongst the most powerful tools that exist today to create a bold future. You also have the life experience, skills, beliefs, and perspective to create a bold future by solving complex global challenges facing humanity.

- Can you name your most meaningful and impactful life experiences?

- Which of your skills do you most enjoy using?

- Do you believe in something so much that you would fall on your sword for it?

- What's your perspective on why your and other people's voices matter in creating a world that you want to live in?

- Which of the United Nations Sustainable Development Goals do you feel most strongly about? **www.sdgs.un.org/goals**

CHAPTER 2

HUMANITY

WHY DOES HUMANITY MATTER?

This is an important question to consider when developing your point of view on why *anything* matters!

The following is how I answer the question of why humanity matters, based on my personal experience and non-scientific understanding:

As a collective. Beyond the scientific understanding of how we developed over nine million years, Homo sapiens are a global species, and many of our macro challenges are global and experienced by millions. Being human means an interconnected existence that is continually enhanced by our collective learnings. Our learnings are passed on to new generations and across boundaries, often through storytelling. And this circle of knowledge continually elevates our collective intelligence. A powerful example of this is the *Songlines*, passed down over thousands of years by the *First Nations People of Australia*.

"A Songline represents a verbal story that supersedes time or place but navigates one through land, lore and position within Indigenous Australia society."[1]

As an experience. Beyond the species development of Homo sapiens is an intelligent and energetic experience of being human. There is still so much we don't understand about the human experience, so it's imperative to keep learning and to keep an open mind about what's possible. A human experience

---

1 https://oursonglines.com/our-team/

can include a combination of sensing, emotion, compassion, intuition, creativity, thoughts, feelings, beliefs, values, and how we behave.

As creators. Here are just a few remarkable examples of what humans have created in the past several thousand years:

The entire timeline of human evolution is around nine million years. The oldest Homo sapiens date back three hundred thousand years. The behavioural and cognitive traits that distinguish current Homo sapiens from other anatomically modern humans, hominids, and primates occurred fifty thousand years ago.

Stonehenge was built around five thousand years ago; the Great Wall of China around two thousand seven hundred years ago; and the Roman Colosseum is less than two thousand years old.

And more recently, in 1879, Thomas Edison invented the light bulb; in 1897, Isaac Newton published his comprehensive theory of gravity; in 1903, the Wright Brothers made their first powered flights; in 1916, Albert Einstein published his theory of general relativity; and, in 2007, Apple released the first iPhone; to name just a few of the incredible innovations created by inspired humans.

For the past several decades, some would argue that we've used humans to do repetitive work; work that robots will do in the future, to free up our innate potential for creativity and our emotional, connected experience of life.

We are innovating all the time: the future is ours to create.

"As far as we know, humans have the unique power of forethought: the ability to imagine the future in many possible iterations and then to actually create the future we imagine. Forethought also allows humans generative and creative abilities unlike those of any other species."[2]

WHAT DO GEN Z AND MILLENNIALS THINK ABOUT HUMANITY?

Humans are hardwired to make *progress*. Making progress towards a better life, community, or world is a universal human trait, and we naturally aspire to achieve a life of meaning and purpose.

How do people around the world define *better*?

They define *better life* as wanting to be healthy and happy. For example: if I am personally healthy and happy, then I am strong, and I have the energy to pay it forward and help create a better community.

Better community is often defined as people being able to improve the lives of their family and the people with whom they share a local area. This includes building trust, a safer community, and living by the values that drive a community to pull together to create equality for all.

Better world is deeply, passionately, and articulately expressed as a future and a planet that support humanity. A world in which humans and nature live synergistically and are in a relationship

---

2 Marder, Lisa. "What Makes Us Human?" ThoughtCo, Aug. 27, 2020, thoughtco.com/what-makes-us-human-4150529.

with each other. A world in which humans take only what they need, allowing all life to thrive.

Through many conversations with Gen Z and millennials around the world, what I've learned is that in times of unprecedented disruption and unpredictability, people embrace a human-first world. They crave real, human experiences based on values that create purpose and progress towards a better life. People want to connect with people they trust: close members of their community including their parents, friends, and teachers. They judge the brands they interact with through the lens of human values, and trust is paramount.

Gen Z and millennials believe their responsibility is to create a better future for humanity and the planet. They expect brands to do what it takes to support their consumer in their desire to create a better future for humanity. For example, they ask companies to make technology useful, by which they mean to solve significant problems.

In leveraging modern-day, human-made tools, for example technology, brands are expected to do more than extract snippets of user data and aggregate it for their self-interest. People are asking for brands to create and share useful data-driven insights that can help humanity make progress towards a better world. They desire to collaborate with brands whose values they resonate with and who they trust; brands who understand the mission to create a better future for all.

Humans have created most of the problems that we are now trying to solve. Planet earth does not create problems to trip us up! Our planet would be fine without humans living on it, and as far as we know, it doesn't need us to survive. So, as the leading protagonist in this age of the Anthropocene[3], humans must figure out how to live synergistically with one another and with nature.

"Humans are both unique and paradoxical. While they are the most advanced species intellectually, technologically, and emotionally—extending human lifespans, creating artificial intelligence, traveling to outer space, showing great acts of heroism, altruism, and compassion—they also have the capacity to engage in primitive, violent, cruel, and self-destructive behavior."[4]

Gen Z, in particular, feel like humanity has reached a watershed moment at which we must collaborate across boundaries to survive and thrive.

---

3 The Anthropocene Epoch is an unofficial unit of geologic time, used to describe the most recent period in Earth's history when human activity started to have a significant impact on the planet's climate and ecosystems. https://www.nationalgeographic.org/encyclopedia/anthropocene/

4 Marder, Lisa. "What Makes Us Human?" ThoughtCo, Aug. 27, 2020, thoughtco.com/what-makes-us-human-4150529.

WHAT DO *YOU* THINK ABOUT WHY HUMANITY MATTERS?

The question of who we are and who we want to be is important. It's easy to get caught up in a wave of beliefs handed down to us through our family, community, society, and culture that solidify into *that's just the way it is*. Taking the opportunity to step back and reflect gives us the space to create a new framework and to move forward with a fresh sense of purpose and meaning.

Imagine if every human had a sense of deep connection to humanity. Imagine the collective drive to solve the problems that threaten our future survival. From that grounded, wise, and loving place, they would create an effective way of passing on knowledge to help the next generation, who would in turn help the following generation to thrive.

Coming full circle, as the leader of a brand with sometimes unimaginable resources, it's so important you spend some time thinking about your interpretation of humanity and the role that you can play. I believe we are all here to play the biggest role we can. If you don't know where you stand, it's difficult to invest your time and energy in future thinking. It's also hard to authentically encourage people to believe in the value of working towards a better future and beyond a short-term-gain mindset.

We are living in a time when old systems (built by humans as a reflection of what we believed we needed in the past) are being disrupted. World order, natural order, and human values are now aggressively challenged. As a leader of a brand, it's important to define your personal values and purpose, before defining the values and role of the brand you lead.

Our individual values are as diverse and as unique as each of us. Our values are "principles that you hold to be of worth in your life"[5].

Our values live deep within us and they guide us on how we want to live our life, and help us understand the role we might play in creating a bold future. Being clear on our values also helps others trust us because our actions align with our words, and we are authentic. As a leader with a point of view on the direction in which humanity must travel, trust is essential to inspire people to follow you.

---

5 Co-Active Training Institute, California.

COACHING QUESTIONS

People can interpret the word humanity as lofty and out of reach. In contrast, I believe it is a very grounded and practical word. To me, it means all human life and how we refer to ourselves and behave as a collective.

If we don't give an identity to our collective whole, it gives us an excuse to dehumanise others and minimise the problems that they face. From that place, how will we connect with solving the problems that affect our collective ability to survive, and hopefully thrive?

If we treat each other with kindness, stay curious about each other's diverse perspectives and uplift each other's unique strengths, could we solve problems more effectively?

- What's your opinion?

CHAPTER 3

FUTURE

When speaking to people about the future, I've noticed their perspectives vary widely. They say things like:

- You can't predict the future.

- The future is now.

- The future is not preordained.

- The future has already been decades in the making.

- My hopes and dreams are my future.

I think of the future as a period of time yet to come which provides us with a wonderful opportunity to build a bridge between our present reality and our vision for a new one.

Open access to the high-fidelity information all around us means that it's reasonable to suggest we *can* see the current trajectory of our macro-level future for the next twenty years with some clarity. Some examples include:

- Despite the pandemic, the economy will continue to grow.

- Technological innovation will enable exponential development of artificial intelligence.

- Climate change will continue to impact people's access to basic resources.

- Geo-political collaboration will help to solve global challenges.

- The increasing global population will put pressure on biodiversity.

- Investors will pour billions into innovation.

- Democracy will continue to jostle with autocracy.

- Scientists predict more global health pandemics.

- People will fight to stay in control in the face of unprecedented high-speed change.

- Industry will continue to drive people to work harder, and to reward them less for their efforts.

Each of these scenarios leads to a myriad of possible outcomes, and I believe we can already see enough to take responsibility for the choices we make about how we want things to develop. We will cover more about macrotrends and how they relate to brands in the next chapter.

BEING FUTURISTIC

The future is what we make it. It's up to us to do all we can to tilt the odds in our favour to create the future we want. When speaking to young people, they talk eloquently about various time horizons from today to several generations ahead. They talk of solutions to problems and what it might take to achieve them. Humans have the innate gift of tapping into their imagination to create pictures in their mind, and it's fun to world-build with those who use the gift for positive visions of the future. Their wisdom, energy, ambition, and spirit are inspiring. Nothing seems impossible. Challenging, yes, but not impossible.

If we made something in the past that no longer works for us, we can change it for the future. People fear change – for many it feels risky and creates resistance, especially when they perceive things to be going *well enough*. They don't want to risk disrupting the status quo. When weighing up the consequences of making change, we must also consider the cost of not changing and adapting.

"Well, all stories about the future are actually about the now...1984 was actually about 1948 and looking down the road what might happen should England become like the Soviet Union of the now. So the Handmaid's Tale was about trends that were already there in the now event, and what might happen if those trends continued on in that way. Would we like that? Is that where we want to live?"

Margaret Atwood, author of *The Handmaid's Tale*

As a brand leader with a great deal of resources at your fingertips, it's important to reflect upon whether you're compelled to nudge the future in a particular direction in alignment with where you believe the world needs to go, where macrotrends and society are pointing, or whether you are content to ride the wave of short-term tactics for reliable profit.

People now expect brands to take a stand and will call them out as imposters when they make empty promises about *purpose* and *vision* without backing them up with meaningful action. Meaningful action may require risking profits to make progress, or the brand will be judged as inauthentic.

Thoughtfully and strategically reorienting the power of your brand towards a longer-term horizon means you can move forward with confidence – and so can everyone else in your business. Some brands are already doing an outstanding job, looking out into the future, finding new opportunities, and delivering on their vision and strategy. Many more brands are developing their strategy and adapting their actions quickly. Others have yet to commit to creating sincere long-term value for their spectrum of stakeholders. Next-generation brand leaders hold the keys to a bold future for humanity and they must decide what to do next.

Creating the future is not a mystery. Every action we take today shapes tomorrow in some way. It's easy to believe creating a better future is someone else's job, or that it's impossible, but we all have the power to take action. We don't need to wait for permission. To make a difference, we only need to take small daily steps in the direction we feel is right. One minute from now is already the future, so the future begins in this moment!

Sometimes, as creators, we don't know where to start, but the best way forward is just to begin. Things will happen that you would never expect or predict, and you can only decide what to do when you face the reality of the situation.

Over the past two years many things have converged, collided, and challenged our relative stability and pattern of growth. We must remember to be intentional about what happens on the other side of significant disruption, like the pandemic. Humans have proven over thousands of years that two of our core skills are adaptability and creativity. Gen Z and millennials are already creatively adapting and collectively adjusting through this constantly changing context. People are innately adaptable and creative, and we will always rise to the challenge.

BEING CREATIVE

Humans are natural born creators. We needed to be creative to survive this long. We create art and science and solutions to problems all day, every day. Sometimes we create something from nothing; other times we create and build on something that already exists. Creativity is empowering and powerful. It gives us some control over what we want to see come to life.

In contrast to our native state of being creative, this age of industrialisation has required workers to be on production lines and in offices to fuel growth. As Gen Xers growing up in the Western world, we've been trained to play a role in a free market economic system. It appears our lives were supposed to play out like this: be born, be educated, climb the corporate ladder, get married, get a mortgage, have kids, retire, travel, die.

We were not trained to find and unleash our purpose. We were not encouraged to be original, use our strengths and our imagination, or think creatively. We didn't consider our impact on the world around us. Our children still learn and repeat formulas in school.

Upon reflection of my own experience, it's hard not to feel like a cog in the wheel when you look at it this way. We are still expected to be content with our individual achievements in what some would call *the capitalist rat race*. A compliant workforce making some personal progress towards a better life is easier for the traditional powers that be to control, and efficiency works well for an industrial capitalist system.

Of course, there have been some incredible macro-level benefits to this capitalist system. Since the last world war, through multilateral efforts, we have enjoyed a backdrop of peace and democracy, and a stable geo-political world order, and many millions of people have been lifted out of poverty around the world.

On the flip side, this system has also created a depth of inequality that has been barely understood and which has held so many generations of people back globally. There is so much latent talent we have still to unlock in our quest to unite and create a better world.

While technological innovation is a certainty and will replace some of the work people do today[6], humans develop creative intelligence over time. There isn't an app for that! It requires people everywhere to have the opportunity to nurture curiosity and diversity of thought, to have a variety of life experiences and to gain exposure to different cultures. It requires an environment where we value listening to others. Limiting ourselves by only listening to the same voices doesn't contribute to the diversity needed to become an organisation brimming with creative intelligence.

Giving people an opportunity to develop and voice their unique strengths and original perspectives opens the way for creativity and innovation. Luckily for our collective futures, highly motivated Gen Z and millennials desire to rethink almost everything and to create the future from the ground up. As brand leaders, how will we support these creators who want to build this bold future?

---

6 https://www.weforum.org/centre-for-the-fourth-industrial-revolution/areas-of-focus

"Creativity is intelligence having fun" is a phrase often
attributed to Einstein.[7]

The World Economic Forum names creativity, originality, and initiative in the top skills needed in the next decade[8], alongside analytical thinking and innovation, complex problem solving, critical thinking, and analysis.

However, enterprise leaders interviewed for this book called out several barriers to creative thinking:

- personal limiting beliefs

- fear of the unknown and fear of failure

- flying below the radar to stay safe and employed

- creating change at scale is not easy

- corporate politics means risk of exclusion from peer group

- lack of direction or prioritised resources from leadership

- lack of permission, time, space, and incentive

By being intentional about creating the right environment, we can take proactive steps towards creating a bold future which we believe will progress humanity or nature positively.

It won't always be easy, and we will need to face fears and to conquer many challenges. But if we believe in the vision, trust in ourselves and in our natural optimism and resourcefulness, it will help us make that future real.

---

7 https://www.bbc.com/culture/article/20210105-why-being-creative-is-good-for-you?ocid=ww.social.link.email

8 https://www.weforum.org/reports/the-future-of-jobs-report-2020/in-full

BEING BOLD

Bold is a strong word. It can be interpreted by people as good or bad. It can be wildly motivating for some and drastically off-putting for others.

Those who find the word bold motivating typically equate it with big, brave, ambition, audacity, gravitas, hope, optimism, exponential thinking. It's inspiring and energising.

Those who find it off-putting typically associate it with risk, with it being hard to make a difference on your own. It creates instability, uncertainty, and hurt feelings. It leads to being jaded from the pressure society demands on our time, and incremental thinking. People find it exhausting to think of how much effort it would take, so they give up before they begin.

Creating a bold future is not for everyone, but everyone should have the opportunity to realise their hopes and dreams for a better life and world.

My intention in using the word bold is to provoke us to think bigger; to take courageous steps to deliver something new, beyond the obvious; to create substantive shifts towards impact and fulfilment, and a better life, community, and world. Bold can be as big or as small as you like and because it's a simple process, anyone can do it.

Bold can mean being intentional, useful, purposeful, value-driven, and giving our life and work meaning. I use it to check in with myself that I am making the biggest difference I can. It pushes me to the edge of what I believe I am capable of, and then pushes me some more. It asks me to trust myself, the universe, and the people around me. It's not always emotionally easy to be bold. It can take bravery, hard work, and a deep breath to steady yourself when you make tough choices, but that's where I feel most alive and where my life is meaningful. Isn't that the point of it all?

COACHING QUESTIONS

The future hasn't happened yet. But some kind of future is guaranteed to arrive, whether we want it to or not!

- Since the future is ours to influence, what kind of future do you dream of for yourself, for those around you and for those that share your planet?

- Do you dare to boldly breathe life into those dreams of the future by writing them down or sketching them out?

CHAPTER 4

BRANDS

In a complex and divided world, global brands are untapped catalysts in creating a future that works for all of us.

A BRAND BURGER

Imagine, if you will, the layers of a veggie burger. The top half of the bun represents governments. Next, a slice of cheese represents multilateral agencies. The veggie burger represents global brands, and the bottom half of the bun represents over seven billion citizens of the world. The component parts, while tasty on their own, do not make a complete burger.

Let's break down the role of each component and the potential for brands to become the feature ingredient in creating a bold future.

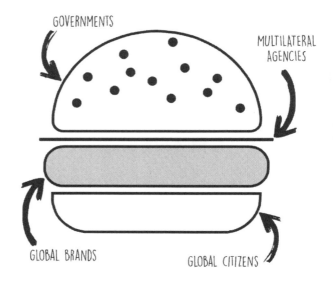

GOVERNMENTS

One role of governments is to architect a vision for the future (for example, develop policy and law to achieve net-zero carbon emissions by 2050[9]) and to provide infrastructure and an environment that enable citizens to prosper, and civil society to function effectively. It's well documented that governments haven't been in good standing with the citizens of the world for some time. The perceived role of politicians being in charge is seen by many as conflicting with doing the right thing for their citizens and the planet.

---

9 https://www.bbc.com/news/science-environment-54858638

MULTILATERAL AGENCIES

Since the Second World War, the role of multilateral agencies has been to enable collaboration across three or more nations to solve shared global problems and to defend democratic values within a competitive geo-political context (for example, eradicate poverty, combat global health challenges, and prevent global conflicts). While these agencies have done monumental work and made significant progress against post-war priorities, these organisations themselves also recognise that they must "regain their legitimacy and widespread appeal"[10]. Moving forward, multilateral organisations such as the World Economic Forum clearly call out the need to reset global collaboration between all stakeholders (governments, companies, and civil society) to "address the economic, environmental, social and technological challenges of our complex, interdependent world"[11].

GLOBAL BRANDS

Inherently, global brands cross geographical, philosophical, and cultural boundaries. Uniquely, the biggest brands have the resources to bring people with shared vision and values together and to mobilise change through their voice on a scale large enough to make a significant difference in the areas they focus on.

---

10 https://www.weforum.org/agenda/2020/07/government-global-models-multilateralism-financial-capitalism/
11 https://www.weforum.org/events/the-davos-agenda-2021/

Any experience that someone has with your brand *is* the brand. The experience should reflect the highest intention and values of the brand. As we have covered earlier in the book, people not only expect brands to be built on strong values, but they will gravitate towards brands built on values that resonate with their own.

Values are as diverse and unique as each of us. Values reflect our beliefs and priorities; they manifest in who we are and in the things we do. Our values live deep inside us; they guide us on how we want to live our life and they help us understand the role we might play in the world. Being clear on our values also helps people trust in our authenticity.

As a brand or a leader with a clear vision for the future, being declarative about what you stand for and taking aligned action builds trust, which is an essential criterion to inspire people to engage with you.

A global brand holds the power to influence many stakeholders (for example, governments, other companies, and civil society) and has the potential to become much more than a capitalist generator of profit. Many global brands play a significant role in people's lives and can be with them through most life stages. In my conversations with Gen Z and millennials, they told me they see global brands as global citizens. Not only do they hold brands responsible for their actions, but they hold them accountable to the same set of human values to which they'd hold a friend accountable: trust, transparency, authenticity, and empathy.

Brands used to be seen as a vehicle for recognition and recall, a promise of value or quality, or a logo on a product advertisement. The role of a brand has evolved and is now viewed by many as a catalyst for change. Brands have an opportunity to build the bridge between today and tomorrow, and to proactively use their vision, values, and voice to create a bold future.

GLOBAL CITIZENS

Seven billion people on the planet choose how to unleash whatever spending power they have, based on what's important to them. Gen Z and millennials have made it clear that they will make their future purchase decisions based on whether a brand lives up to the ethical challenge of creating a positive impact.

THE ROLE OF A BRAND THROUGH THE EYES OF GEN Z AND MILLENNIALS

- Comes alongside you to support you as you journey through life.

- Solves a particular problem at no detriment to humanity and the planet.

- Recognises you on a human level.

- Is in a relationship with you, based on human values: trust, transparency, authenticity, and empathy.

- Stands for something and fights for what's right, together with their consumer or user.

- Understands you so that it can serve you personally.

WHAT'S NEXT FOR CATALYST BRANDS?

By my calculation, there are five billion Gen Z and millennials in the world today. Together, these two generations represent approximately sixty-three per cent of the global population.

The priorities of this group are to solve mental health challenges, climate change, and problems which create inequality. They have been vocal in their challenges to the people in power – government, multilateral agencies, and brands – for quite some time. But so far, change has been very slow, as eloquently summed up by Greta Thunberg's speech at Davos 2021[12].

In April 2021, the top 50 global brands[13] in the world are roughly (because values are constantly changing) equal in size, at $3.025 trillion dollars, to the fifth largest economy in the world, as measured by nominal GDP by the International Monetary Fund[14]. Theoretically, this means that the collective influence of, and the opportunity for, brands to play a bigger role in creating the future is potentially colossal.

While the events of 2020 and 2021 created an opportunity for a great deal of soul searching, the collective conversation around creating a better future has really only just begun. Some brands have started to tie their executive compensation to their emerging people, planet, and profit goals[15]. But in talking with many CEOs, lack of clarity around incentive to change is currently holding them back from embracing a different way of leveraging their brand.

---

12 https://www.weforum.org/agenda/2021/01/greta-thunberg-message-to-the-davos-agenda/
13 https://brandirectory.com/rankings/global/table
14 https://worldpopulationreview.com/countries/countries-by-gdp
15 https://news.nike.com/news/fy20-nike-inc-impact-report-ceo-letter

Other brands are beginning to flex their muscles on important issues and as a result they are taking a lot of heat from politicians and consumers for either taking a stand or not taking a strong enough stand for a better world; for example, when Coca-Cola and Delta stood up for voting rights in Georgia[16], and when Nike and H&M were boycotted in China because they removed cotton sourced from China from their supply chains over concerns of alleged forced labour in cotton production[17].

In my opinion, these brands are doing exactly what they should be doing, by beginning to take a stand on behalf of their consumers by challenging the status quo and assumptions that have been made in the past. This shift in power will undeniably result in a certain amount of turbulence in the coming years until we (society) are collectively happy enough with our new direction.

In summary, many global brands began life as a start-up and evolved over decades to become the power-players they are today. Brands have been created purposely to play a huge role in our lives so that we become reliant upon them. The global pandemic has challenged society to ask big questions about where we find ourselves in this stage of our own evolution and has given us an opportunity to reconsider how we want to shape our collective future. Brands have an opportunity to consider the same and to redefine the role they want to play and how they can use their untapped power for the benefit of a better world.

---

16 https://www.nytimes.com/2021/04/05/business/voting-rights-ceos.html?refer-ringSource=articleShare
17 https://www.bbc.com/news/world-asia-china-56519411

COACHING QUESTIONS

In a complex and divided world, brands have the influence and resources to bring people together with shared vision and values and to mobilise change on a scale large enough to make a significant difference.

- Are your personal values aligned with those of your brand?

- As a leader of a brand, who are you serving?

- What do *you* believe is the opportunity for your brand to play a role in creating a bold future?

CHAPTER 5

INSIGHT

Leaders of brands naturally prefer to focus upstream on the creation of an inspiring vision, developing an original strategy, and coaching their team to deliver results.

The reality is they spend much of their time having to deal with so much intrinsic noise before they can define and create long-term meaning for their brand.

Noise might come from lack of clarity on vision, strategic misalignment, short-term volatility, or a shortening of the strategic horizon because of external forces, organisational politics, process issues, resource challenges, their own self-talk – the list goes on.

Finding the time to raise your head and ask questions such as *where are we now?* can feel awkward to the leader challenging the conventional wisdom inside an organisation. But before you create your vision and develop your strategy, it's essential to understand the true context that your brand operates within so you can develop an assured intention about where you are going.

In his book, *Create the Future: Tactics for Disruptive Thinking*, Jeremy Gutsche writes,

"The average lifespan of a large company has fallen from 75 years in the 1950s to 15 years today. If you look at the Fortune 500 companies from the year 2000, over 52% are now gone or displaced and that rate of disruption is accelerating. Ironically, the companies that should be the best at innovation are the same companies that often fail."

While his point explicitly refers to innovation, I wonder how many leaders of global brands are as intentional about investing time in creating the future as they are about leading with agility on a quarter-by-quarter basis. Extraordinary pandemic circumstances excepted, how many would ordinarily lead the brand for long-term relevancy and direct their resources towards solving global problems?

The growth opportunities for some companies are logically finite. Eventually, markets do become saturated, and companies only focused on delivering the same products and services over the short term may stunt their growth potential.

To secure a long-term future, leaders must take a breath and explore their macro context to discover new opportunities for a long-term trajectory. When leaders are experienced in considering the context that affects them, they can be more intentional about the direction of their brand.

Scanning the environment and connecting the dots to develop insight inspires and energises. Being curious opens your eyes, heart, and mind to new information and perspectives, and allows you to see possibilities for your brand in a new light.

By taking a step back and looking at the complete picture, you gain clarity on deciding the best way forward. In my experience there's not enough emphasis on understanding the macrotrends and the world around us to help put the current position of the consumer and the potential of the brand into context.

MACROTRENDS INSIGHT

Fundamental forces shape the world over the long term. Macrotrends include demographic, political, economic, socio-cultural, technological, and ecological shifts that involve large populations, observed at scale, which create long-lasting impact. Macrotrends don't exist in a vacuum. They are deeply intertwined and connected with one another. Getting a feel for macro context is key for you to understand what role your brand plays and what problems it solves for people to make progress.

The very essence of macro means that you will never know or understand everything that's happening in the world, but just because you can't see it, or don't know about it, doesn't mean it's not happening.

The pragmatic approach is to cultivate and maintain a broad interest in macro forces. The most relevant forces, *of the moment*, show up in everyday news, culture, and trend reports. And if you dig deeper into the bigger picture of an area which intrigues you, it can get really fascinating. It's easy for society to get pulled along in the flow of macrotrends without recognising the greater significance.

Your role is to join the dots at a high level so you can identify patterns and observe the bigger picture. In taking the time out of your busy day to do this, it will better equip you to predict the future.

Some leaders hold the view it's best to respond to what's happening in culture in real time. It comes down to how you see your role as a leader of a powerful and influential brand with potentially millions of dollars to spend on changing people's behaviour, and the part you wish to play in shaping the future for the next decade.

My belief is we control our destiny, and that the future is ours to create. I think we should encourage brands to play an intentional role in creating a future inspired by their highest values.

CONSUMER INSIGHT

Walking a mile in your consumers' shoes, to understand the world around them and how they see themselves fitting into it, is vital. A brand leader's role is to get under the skin of their consumers' culture, perspective, their experience of their daily lives, their motivations, values, hopes, and dreams, their community and connections, the problems they need solving, and why they are significant.

When you understand what stops them from achieving what they want, you can break down the barrier and help them progress.

I see the role of a brand leader as being like that of an anthropologist. You need to meet your consumers where they are, not where you are. Watch, listen, and learn. Be endlessly curious about understanding the unspoken: their energy, movement, and behaviour.

Only by learning how they experience their reality will you develop a clear understanding of, and empathy for, their problems and the role your brand can play in solving them. In spending time with people, they will both implicitly and explicitly tell you exactly what they want and expect of your brand, and the role it can play in helping them.

Understanding what's happening with your consumer and the world around them also helps you to explain credibly the *why* behind your vision. The end user may not be the same person who makes the purchase decision, and so it's useful to understand what the purchaser thinks, feels, and believes too.

EXECUTIVE LEADERSHIP INSIGHT

The goal is to explore what your leaders believe, and their thoughts about the future of the brand, and to understand their motivation to evolve the vision and strategy when things are already going well.

I enjoy interviewing executive leaders because they love to share their thoughts, and it's fun learning about different perspectives of a brand.

Interviewing executive leaders or board members is important for two reasons. The first is you discover what your company leaders think and believe about the world, the role of the brand, the users' experience, and much more.

The second is you get to compare these perspectives to the consumers' opinions and experiences.

Besides hearing what the leaders of your company have to say about your brand and their experience of the world, you will learn about their hopes and dreams for the future, which will help you triangulate all the facts and manage expectations when you build your next brand vision and strategy.

As you move through these steps, these executive interviews will highlight if there is a chasm of understanding and an expectation or a gap between the executive leadership team, the brand, and the consumer.

BUSINESS INSIGHT

Think about your business: the reason it was created, the culture, the vision, the strategy, the positioning of your brand, the performance science, the marketplace data, what's working, and what's not working.

I encourage you to pull reports from as many functions as you can to understand exactly how the business is structured and the reality of how the sales and profit are structured. If you're used to running a P&L (profit and loss), don't assume you already know the answers and what you see is what you get. Typically, the more senior you become, the further away from the truth you are.

It's common practice that people within the organisation will compile reports to show the business in the most favourable light, not in the light that shows you reality. It's natural they want to impress you as their leader, but be sure to ask questions.

Ask for the reports to be sliced in different ways. Look at the business from different perspectives and cross-tabulate what you see until you are happy you can see reality – warts and all.

Do the resources align with the problem your company is trying to solve? Don't be afraid to dig in further. Be sure you truly understand what's happening. Make sure you interview employees at all levels and in as many functions as possible to get a full picture of the situation based on their experience. Make it safe for them to give you honest feedback. And when you gather all of this data, you will spot any gaps.

MARKETPLACE INSIGHT

There is nothing more enlightening than visiting the physical locations where you sell your products or services. Walk around the stores and talk to the retail staff and join them online. Work in the stores for two weeks to get a front-line perspective.

Meet the consumers and speak to people who buy and use your products or services. Talk to them while they are using them in real time. Is your brand solving their problems? What is their experience of your brand?

Don't spend all of your time with your peers as your experience will become too curated and they will only show you a narrow spectrum of reality in its best light. Don't be afraid to face up to reality or it will catch up with you when it's too late to anticipate and fix problems.

INDUSTRY INSIGHT

Are you leading or following the industry? You can learn a lot from marketplace and trend reports and by monitoring what's happening in your industry. Read. Follow. Speak to your peers. Join forums and attend conferences. Listen to podcasts. There is a lot of brilliant content out there for you to immerse yourself in.

I encourage you to reflect on what you learn. Jot down your thoughts to compile a picture of what's happening in your industry. Once you open up this channel of thought, you'll experience a flow of new insights, because that's how the mind works.

DATA INSIGHT

Companies love data because it can help them grow by driving productivity, efficiency, scale, and frequency of purchase, and to develop an efficient value chain end-to-end, including agile inventory management.

It helps them to serve the marketplace and consumers at scale and with speed, to develop actionable insights to create better performing products and services, to anticipate what people need and when, and to deliver engaging content that connects communities.

Consumers love data when it makes their lives easier, for example personalised search results and recommendations, or speed of purchase and delivery. Consumers are understandably concerned about their data falling into the wrong hands and data collection methods infringing on their privacy.

The converging experiences of 2020 and 2021 have catalysed digital transformation around the world. No doubt data will speed up company growth strategies, but in the consumer's mind, data is only as good as its ability to help people make progress towards a better life, community, and world.

Many consumers are not convinced brands understand how to handle and use data for the greater good, and this causes friction.

Ultimately, brands should understand what data they collect and for what purpose. When you have clarity on this, you know how to interrogate the data.

Some examples you may be interested to investigate might include consumer segmentation, pricing analysis, product mix, service engagement, profitability of certain franchises, performance marketing, or scientific performance data.

What does your data tell you about the current position of your brand?

BRAND INSIGHT

Brand leaders can feel emotionally and personally connected to their brand, and hearing uncomplimentary things about it can cause some people to stop listening or become defensive, almost as if it was an indictment of themselves.

It's imperative that leaders are open to discovering and accepting all stakeholder perspectives on what the brand stands for. In doing so, leaders give the brand control of its destiny and a solid foundation on which to take strides forward. Brand insight is not limited to what a leader alone believes.

The richest and most helpful brand insight lies in the hardest truths and it takes raw courage to dig up and shine a light on the truth. Being a truth-teller is not an easy role to play, but it's rewarding in the end.

What does your brand stand for in the minds of all its stakeholders?

Where does the brand fit emotionally, functionally, creatively, spiritually?

In addition to your closest industry competition, everything that competes for time and space in your consumers' lives can be a brand competitor. For example, a gaming brand might compete with an outdoor brand. A social media brand might compete with a music brand.

What other brands take up time and space in the lives of your consumers?

What role does each brand play in your consumers' lives?

Your company may be a brand. Your company may house a portfolio of brands. Your brand may also have sub-brands. Some sub-brands are stronger than the master brand or company brand.

Do you know how the brands and sub-brands within your company relate to one another and if they all add up to something bigger?

While brand share data is useful for tracking quantitative market share, for example number one brand in a key city, or particular aspects of the brand over time, such as *most innovative brand*, it might not enable you to understand the human and emotional side of your brand.

How do you track consumer sentiment towards the emotional side of your brand?

I've interviewed internal and external stakeholders who have a clearer perspective on a brand's future potential than its leaders. This can happen when brand leaders become intrinsically focused on managing the business and don't invest the time to understand the role of their brand in the world.

Are you clear on the long-term potential of your brand to play a meaningful role in the future?

There are so many ways to understand the brand you lead and how it relates to the world and your consumer.

What other opportunities do you have to sense check where your brand is today?

PERSONAL INSIGHT

This is perhaps *the* most significant type of insight.

A spiderweb of macro-level information is extremely useful, but *it doesn't build a vision for the future on its own.* Your life experience and professional expertise, global and strategic perspective, well-honed intuition, and clarity on your role in the world are critical to turn this complex web into tangible priorities.

From this snapshot of the world at a macro level, you can paint a picture of where your brand is today and join the dots to articulate any themes, any barriers to break down, or any problems to solve.

You can identify the insights most relevant to your consumer and specify the advantage your brand has in creating the future.

With this simple, original, and insightful point of view, you can create an inspiring vision, strategic clarity, tangible priorities, and engaging communication that will harness the energy of your brand and team and propel them into their bold future.

COACHING QUESTIONS

Making time and creating space to understand *where are we now?* is the starting point to answering the questions *where do we want to get to?* and *how will we get there?*

Insights can give you a snapshot of where you are now so that you can develop an assured point of view about where you are going next.

Insights open your eyes, heart, and mind to new information and perspectives and allow you to see possibilities for your brand in a new light.

- Are you open to exploring the world surrounding your brand and where your brand is positioned now?

- Are you open to discovering meaningful problems that need to be solved, even if they challenge the status quo?

- How could you begin to generate insights?

CHAPTER 6

VISION

Some people believe they have no control over creating the future and so there's no point creating a vision. I doubt you think that way or you wouldn't be reading this book.

Based on conversations with bold leaders, you believe that a vision embodies the intentional difference you will make in your own life and in the world. You know that a version of the future will happen regardless of any action you take, but you believe in taking considered and deliberate action to create a better future. You appreciate that every day that passes without a vision pushes away the possibility of achieving a bold future. Leaders of powerful brands recognise a deep calling to do what they can to create a better world.

It's true we cannot control the unfolding events of each day, but having a vision is about believing we have an opportunity to approach each day with purpose, to cultivate a sense of awareness of the direction in which we wish to travel to our desired destination. Holding that destination lightly in our consciousness and adapting as we grow empowers us to embrace every moment along the way.

A vision guides us to progress towards something better. It helps us to round up the disparate pieces of our imagination and make sense of them so they become actionable. It represents hope and optimism. A vision can be bold, inspiring, and motivational and tap into a fundamental essence of being human – creativity.

I learned through thousands of hours of coaching conversations with creatively minded people that most are optimistic in their dedication to making an impact and wish to see themselves successfully contributing to the future they envision.

They believe in the power, potential, and purpose of their brand to create a better future. Energised and empowered people are the ones who change the world.

A powerful brand vision is imbued with a deep resonance. It should serve humanity and the planet first and be right for the brand and business. Successful brand visions are connected to a deep human need and give people goosebumps when they interact with them because they recognise they are engaged in something bigger than themselves. Allow people plenty of opportunities to get involved with your brand vision. Be generous so people can get emotional about your vision. Powerful visions are so compelling, people feel they can reach out and almost touch the new reality.

MAKING TIME AND SPACE

People around the world talk about brands as living beings brought to life by the yin and yang of magic and logic. In corporate speak, this is the art and science.

There is a strong sense that when big brands take a leadership position in the world and say something is possible, then it becomes possible. People yearn for brands to take a stand for possibilities that help them bring their hopes and dreams to life. This is the *magic* of your brand and the power at your fingertips.

The *logic* is the brains of the operation: the running of the business and the delivery of products and services where, when, and how people need them. Most leaders spend their careers in logic, managing and operating a business. Based on conversations with corporate leaders, logic currently absorbs most, if not all, of their attention.

The biggest opportunity for leaders to create a vision of the future is in making time and space to break away from the daily grind to imagine what's possible. When they take a step back, and with the right guidance, they see what their brand can become within the bigger context, and then develop an intentional path to move forward.

When I speak to leaders about creating a bold future, their initial reaction is frequently, 'I have so much to do to get the house in order before I can think about the future.' In reality, this approach is back to front and typically results in slow or no progress towards a bold vision, because the perfect day to think about the future never arrives.

As a leader, it's imperative that you take your team away from their day-to-day responsibilities so that you can focus on creating the future. Some leaders feel comfortable committing to quarterly time together and combine creating the future with delivering results. Alternatively, they might combine inspirational contextual or marketplace immersion with team building. Other leaders build mind-bending creative thinking sessions involving once-in-a-lifetime experiences.

The most mind-bending offsite event I attended included a private performance by the Master Mentalist Lior Suchard, in Las Vegas. I will be forever grateful to my boss for that experience – my interpretation of the possibilities in life hasn't been the same since. **www.liorsuchard.com**

BUILDING A VISION WITH YOUR TEAM

As we navigate post-pandemic life, there are many parallels between leaders wanting a more meaningful career for themselves and wanting a more meaningful role for their brand.

Before the pandemic of 2020, there was a sense for many that the demands of society and career filled every single crevice of time with a task or responsibility. But throughout the pandemic, many people have reflected on deeper questions such as how they spend their time, how they want to live their lives, and what they want out of their remaining time on earth.

Now, we can ask the same questions about our brands. What is the most meaningful role for our brands? How can brands help humanity to build the future we want?

Building a vision can be an insightful, collaborative, creative, and fulfilling experience. Spending time with other people exploring their perspective and intuition, connecting the dots with insights you've uncovered, and defining the way forward together is a rare joy.

Building a vision can be done in many ways. You are only limited by your imagination. Understanding the talents and preferences of your team will help you build the right process, experience, and expression.

In bringing a vision to life, I have found that people who know the power of a creative, innovative or problem-solving mindset respond to a combination of visualisation, storytelling, and 'from-to' statements.

Examples of visualisation might include an artist illustration, a film, a rendering, or a mood board. Examples of storytelling might include a manifesto, a news report, or editorial content written as if in the future. A from-to statement can include as much or as little as you like and will articulate where you are today versus where you want to be.

Within a corporate context, envisioning what's possible for your brand is a perfect exercise to do with your team, but without the heavy constraints of judgement, immediate return on investment, or an engagement metric. Everyone in your team brings a unique perspective which the brand can benefit from. I encourage you to let your vision be as big and as bold as you dare.

Creating a shared vision is not a gratuitous and meaningless exercise. If you, the leader, don't have a vision – if you can't or don't desire to lead the creation of a vision – I urge you to step aside and let someone else lead the way. People can tell when you lack passion and commitment, and we only waste time when we simply go through the motions.

Creating a *shared* vision and a common understanding of why you are heading in a particular direction creates transparency and trust, and will inspire and empower your teams. They will unleash their passion and creativity into their work. Through their sense of ownership of the future, they too will become an informal bridge to the future, integrating their vision into their work and conversations, and naturally helping others to trust in the brand's direction.

Creating a shared vision doesn't have to be limited to only *your* brand and team. As the world's biggest brands gravitate towards the same insights and the same consumer, they naturally share similar data and insights with other brands and organisations, and begin to merge around a shared vision of the future. They could also choose to coalesce around a shared responsibility to use their collective resources to develop fresh ways to serve their consumer and the planet.

Taking the notion of a shared vision to the next level might mean that brands and key stakeholders collaborate as a matter of course with governments, to unite their efforts to break barriers and solve problems for upwards of seven billion people.

An example of this approach in action is the collaborative effort to develop vaccines to fight the COVID-19 pandemic. Pharmaceutical companies shared knowledge and expertise with one another, and governments collaborated with the private sector to fund and innovate multiple rapid responses to the virus. It wasn't a perfect response to a global issue, but it was a huge step forward in illustrating what we can achieve when we work together towards a common goal. We can learn from what worked well and what didn't, and move forward from there.

A different example of this collaborative approach in action is the 1969 moon landing, where President John F. Kennedy committed the United States of America to landing a man on the moon and returning him safely to earth. This was followed in 2021, by NASA (an independent agency of the US federal government) selecting Elon Musk's SpaceX to land the first astronauts on the surface of the moon since 1972.

"Industry analysts said the decision underscores the company, founded by Musk in 2002 with the goal of colonizing Mars, as NASA's most trusted private sector partner."[18]

18 https://www.msn.com/en-us/news/technology/nasa-chooses-spacex-to-take-hu-mans-back-to-moon/ar-BB1fJwpM

If you are interested in learning more about a collaborative approach to solving global problems, I recommend following the World Economic Forum Davos Agenda[19] and listening to their podcast, which can be found at **www.weforum.org/focus/ podcasts**.

THE COLLECTIVE INFLUENCE OF BRANDS

As I shared in Chapter 4, the value of the top fifty brands taken together in 2021 is *roughly* equivalent to the fifth biggest economy (nominal GDP) in the world. Leaders of brands can realise their collective power to galvanise government policy and catalyse humanity to achieve its potential.

If you believe that the boldest vision you can build must fall within the guardrails of current policy, regulation, or governance – developed yesterday to solve yesteryear's problems – as opposed to considering your brand's responsibility to support humankind to achieve transformational progress by 2050, then it's not a vision: it's a strategy to deliver results within current constraints.

I'm not suggesting you break the law. However, a bold vision must ultimately push the edges of current policy, regulation, and governance development and force a conversation about a different way forward that supports society's goals. Society doesn't exist to unquestioningly support government policy.

---

19 https://www.weforum.org/events/the-davos-agenda-2021/?stream=day-one-davos-agenda&stream-item=coming-up-stakeholder-capitalism-building-the-future#stream-header

THE DEFINITION OF A VISION

It's rare to find a common understanding of purpose, vision, mission, values, and strategy. People often mix them up. I think of them as follows:

Purpose: We exist to...

Vision: We envision a world where...

Mission: What we will do to make this future real...

Values: As we are creating the future, we will be...

Strategy: How we will deliver the future...

Below you will find examples of two brilliant brands I admire for their inspirational leadership and positive intentions. Despite taking all the information directly from their websites and reporting, it's still challenging to understand their vision of the future.

EXAMPLE 1: VERIZON

Disclaimer: For illustration purposes only. I'm surmising at the highest level, based on what I see on the website and in publicly available reporting. Verizon employees may hold a completely different perspective, based on their internal knowledge.

Verizon Purpose
We create the networks that move the world forward.[20]

Verizon Vision
(This isn't obvious on Verizon's website, so I am inserting my best guess based on the information available.)
A world where ... the promise of technology enhances "the ability of humans, businesses and society to do more new and do more good".

Verizon Mission
We transform how people, businesses and things connect with each other through innovative communications and technology solutions.[21]

Verizon Values
Integrity. Respect. Performance Excellence. Accountability. Social Responsibility.

Verizon Strategy
(This isn't obvious on Verizon's website, so I am inserting my best guess based on the information available.)
Verizon is transforming how people, businesses and technologies interact, setting the stage for the next Industrial Revolution by:

1. Connecting People and Things through 5G Network / 4G LTE / Broadband & Fibre / Multi-access Edge Computing (MEC)

2. Connecting Business & Industry through Managed Security / Public Safety / Smart Cities / Internet of Things

3. Informing & Entertaining through Verizon Media / Fios TV & Internet

---

20 https://www.verizon.com/about/our-company/who-we-are https://www.verizon.com/about/news/we-create-networks-move-world-forward
21 https://www.verizon.com/about/our-company

EXAMPLE 2: NIKE

Disclaimer: For illustration purposes only. I'm surmising at the highest level, based on what I see on the website and in publicly available reporting. Nike employees may hold a completely different perspective, based on their internal knowledge.

Nike Purpose
To redefine human potential – in the game and around the globe.[22]
Or, to move the world forward through the power of sport.[23]

Nike Vision
(This isn't obvious on Nike's website, so I am inserting a made-up example, based on the information available.)
A world where ... every athlete* has an opportunity through sport to reach their potential in life. *If you have a body, you are an athlete.

Nike Mission
To bring inspiration and innovation to every athlete* in the world. *If you have a body, you are an athlete.

Nike Values
Serve Athletes*. Create the Future of Sport. Be on the Offense Always. Do the Right Thing. Win as a Team.

Nike Strategy
Make Sport a Daily Habit[24] by

1. Accelerating innovation

2. Creating the seamless premium marketplace of the future[25]

3. Introducing 2025 purpose targets[26]

---

22 https://news.nike.com/news/fy20-nike-inc-impact-report-ceo-letter, https://purpose-cms-preprod01.s3.amazonaws.com/wp-content/uploads/2021/03/30191535/FY20-NIKE-Inc.-Impact-Report_Executive-Summary1.pdf
23 https://purpose.nike.com
24 https://news.nike.com/news/nike-digital-health-activity-resources
25 https://s1.q4cdn.com/806093406/files/doc_financials/2021/q3/FY21-Q3-Combined-NIKE-Press-Release-Schedules-FINAL-(003).pdf
26 https://purpose.nike.com/2025-targets

It might *seem* like some brands know what the future will become because they make bold statements such as 'We don't wait for the future. We build it.'[27] But when you look closer, it's hard to distil their vision from the information available. Many are focused on what they do and how they do it.

Is this because, in their heart of hearts, brands essentially see their role as being limited to providing new *capabilities* or *tools* to enable *citizens* of the world to create their own future? Is it that brands don't really want to play a role in creating the future, or is it just that they haven't needed to consider doing much more than making a profit, until now?

Or is it simply that humans in leadership positions are not empowered to be as visionary as we need them to be?

Or they don't have the space and time to create a vision?

Or they don't have a vision of what they want the future to look like and therefore, it's almost impossible to define their role in creating a bold future?

What do you think?

---

27 https://www.verizon.com/about/our-company/who-we-are

LEADING THE CREATION, INTEGRATION, AND COMMUNICATION OF A VISION

One of the key roles of your leadership team is to develop a clear vision that will enable the brand to thrive in a future global context.

Creating an original vision that the rest of the business can get behind is challenging work. As it should be. Taking the world to a new place is an enormous responsibility, with many interconnected consequences.

The expression of a brand vision by the leadership team often gives meaning to why the company exists. As a company grows and change is delivered over time, the vision can evolve to reflect the changing global context within which it operates and to enable the brand and business to stay relevant.

A brand vision has the power to energise and direct all of its company constituents towards the creation of a better world.

Different functions within a company will typically draft off the brand vision and contribute to its achievement through the development of their own strategy and resource planning. If this happens at your company, it's a prerequisite to ensure the component parts of multiple functional strategies ladder up to delivering the singular vision for your brand.

When communicating your brand vision, keep it simple. You will take complex, divergent insights and make sense of them in a way that everyone can understand. This way, you will lead people on a journey when communicating your vision. Make it visceral and attainable. An authentic vision is based on deep insight, not on ideas that just sound good. This means you will be able to articulate clearly the human impact.

Your aim is to create a tangible, consistent, and repeatable message that is meaningful to people. This will build trust in the brand and belief in the impact you will create on the world together.

Given the evolving macro context and the global challenges that will foreseeably surround you and your brand for the next decade or two, the big question for you to consider now is:

Is it time for you to revisit your brand's vision?

COACHING QUESTIONS

A vision guides us to make progress towards something better. It helps us to round up the disparate pieces of our imagination and situation, and make sense of them so they become actionable.

- How can your brand help to build the future we want?

- Are your purpose, vision, mission, values, and strategy clearly defined so that people can join you on this journey and resources easily flow in the right direction?

- What gets in the way of you making time and space to create a bold vision for your brand?

CHAPTER 7

STRATEGY

The role of strategy is to force the prioritisation of initiatives, resources, and action towards the vision in a way that will create value today and in the future.

In this book, we focus on creating value in the future. Value in the future will come in part from resetting the vision and strategy, which enhances society and elevates the value of brands. Remember, brands exist to benefit people, not the other way around. We need to make brands work harder for us, and strategic clarity will allow that to happen.

There is a difference between strategic thinking, strategic planning, and strategic implementation.

STRATEGIC THINKING

Strategic thinking takes a macro, forward-leaning perspective, which allows us to disrupt conventional wisdom positively, to imagine possible new futures, to synthesise complexity into tangible priorities and strategic clarity, and to inform decision-making.

By spending quality time on the insights and vision work upfront, the strategic way forward *almost* writes itself.

The key question evolves from what our strategy should be to whether we have the courage to create the strategy that is asking to be created, and the courage to make the tough decisions needed to make the future real.

It can be intimidating to figure out how to make bold visions happen. Bold visions can paralyse even the most confident and experienced people.

For example, through insight and visioning work, let's imagine it's clear that your consumers and investors want your brand to put climate change at the centre of its efforts.

They want you to use your brand as a trojan horse to change industry and consumer behaviour. Your heart sinks at the thought of such a monumental shift. You and your team have paid with blood, sweat, and tears to deliver your current market leadership position. Forty successful years of history and experience tell you that profitable growth and speed to market cannot be achieved in a climate-friendly way without significant investment and innovation.

This situation puts you in an awkward position. How could you deliver profitable growth and speed to market in a low-carbon, clean-energy way? Is it even possible? These are the types of questions and thinking that can lead to overwhelm and loss of confidence.

A better question to ask to open up possibilities in the unknown is, what could your wild and unconstrained strategy be to achieve the new vision?

To move forward, I recommend you gather a diverse small group to go on this exciting journey together. They must be people who are open to being creative, curious, and courageous, and who will discuss strategic options without judgement or attachment so they can work through the challenges with you.

People with a strong sense of strategic intent and purpose

can typically join the dots and create a unique perspective and advantage that can shape the future of your brand.

Strategic thinkers help big brands to break old paradigms by working within the current system to manifest a new energising vision and fresh direction for the brand.

These people understand the brand and the business, and they know how to poke holes in conventional wisdom that keep the brand stuck in the status quo. They can jolt the system into growth by resetting the direction of the business, repositioning the brand, and validating with the consumer so you can invest your resources to create a bold future with confidence.

The point about breaking paradigms is that sometimes brands get stuck in a particular way of thinking and behaving and it's important to be proactive about disrupting your brand before someone or something else does it for you.

Creating an innovative strategy that will drive the brand and the world forward can be *hard work*. You will need to invest your energy into championing it. It will take passion, perspective, commitment, and perseverance. If it's only a paper exercise that lives in the cloud and is talked about at intermittent meetings, it is unlikely to become the brand's future reality.

Corporate leadership theoretically leads this effort, but, as we know, many leaders can't spare the time to invest in creating the future because they are extremely busy managing the current business and team.

Because of this, there is a high risk that strategic thinking won't happen at all, leaving the company deeply ingrained in its comfort zone. Sometimes busy corporate leaders pass on the vision baton, highlighting the fault lines in the understanding of the role of a leader.

There may be a temptation to bring in consultants to do the strategic thinking and vision creation for you. I urge you to resist.

While external consultants or agencies might add meaningful value in bringing a fresh perspective or taking up the slack on some of the insight and process work that needs to get done, nothing replaces the knowledge you have about the potential of your brand, business, and people when creating the vision for the future of your brand.

Delegating this role and responsibility at such an early stage in the process to an outsider means that the organisation has an excuse to reject ownership of the vision or strategy to create a bold future because that's what you, the leader, did. In my experience, you will open the door to inertia and resistance, which will make progress considerably harder to achieve.

Energy and alignment to create the future at the very top of the organisation is fundamental to intentionally transitioning a vision through the business from end-to-end. Without this energy and alignment, there's little point in moving forward because ownership of the vision must be embedded into individual hearts and minds, and managers must be incentivised to ensure the vision's transition, survival, and success.

STRATEGIC PLANNING

Strategic planning is the process of defining *how* we will deliver the vision, align resources, and communicate effectively to create value for the brand and key stakeholders. The planning process also defines the specific action needed to make the future vision a reality.

There are a multitude of business strategy models, frameworks, and tools available to help companies get organised to deliver their vision. Some brands hire consultants or agencies at this stage to help them define value-creating strategy, to develop human-centred brand innovation and to put the building blocks in place to deliver results.

Working backwards from the vision, strategic planning breaks the vision down into chunks and phases to enable the team to prioritise resources over time. Each phase can be broken down further into specific tasks and each task assigned to an individual so people become accountable for each step. This *chunking down* will naturally result in a roadmap needed to operationalise and implement the work.

It *sounds* simple, but many leaders don't feel empowered to make decisive or bold choices to support delivering the vision or strategy. They feel that current circumstances (often internal politics and the insatiable drive for profitable growth) constrain their decision-making.

Making decisive choices inevitably results in consequences. Mostly, we make decisions because we want *good* consequences to follow. But sometimes, leaders become paralysed by the thought of bad consequences or the personal risk associated with decision-making in large companies.

Whatever the consequential outcome, you have the power to *choose* your perspective and how to embrace it.

The more intentional the choices a leader makes, the more progress the brand will typically make towards achieving its vision.

Making definitive choices in order to deliver the vision and strategy can be fraught with dissonance. The lack of commitment to making clear yes or no decisions is the biggest barrier to successfully delivering any vision, whether personal or professional.

In saying yes to something, what are you saying no to? In saying no to something, what are you saying yes to? Conscious and unconscious fears about the answers to these questions frequently spark indecision and keep people stuck.

Consciously or unconsciously, some company cultures appear to frown upon people who say no. I know of at least three people whose personal leadership identities are literally the word 'yes' because they don't want to be labelled as difficult lest it affect their chances of progression. If that sounds familiar, ask yourself, who is perpetuating this "yes" culture in your business, and why?

While this yes approach sounds positive on the surface, when people are afraid to tell the truth and to say no when something doesn't feel right, the culture can quickly become stagnant and toxic.

Saying yes isn't inherently bad. Yes will sometimes be the right response or it could be an intentional strategy to enable you to take an interesting detour to explore something new without an agenda. But I encourage you not to say yes just because you feel like a victim of your current circumstance or because you feel powerless to say no. Right now, the world faces too many human-made challenges and we cannot afford to shrink our potential, our voice, or our vision by saying yes simply to satisfy others.

Ideally, the corporate strategic planning process will ensure a mechanism to review all concerns and functional strategies together. This ensures that functional strategies are interconnected and ladder up to support the brand's vision to create a bold future.

This process also facilitates a basic level of communication with key stakeholders to ensure functions don't overlook roadblocks or cannibalise one another in the competition for limited resources.

Sometimes brands can't move forward as fast as they would like because they have previous commitments and investments that prevent a new strategy from being adopted. Maybe an old strategy must be combined with or exist alongside a new strategy in order to enable the brand to move forward.

STRATEGIC IMPLEMENTATION

Strategic implementation, or intentional action, produces measurable outcomes.

A roadmap creates focused action. When well managed, it helps people to consistently focus on the bigger things, which increases the odds of your brand creating the biggest impact. Properly operationalised, a roadmap can prevent people doing *busywork* that wastes time and goes nowhere.

By laying out your roadmap against a specific time frame, it's easy to see how the phases of work that deliver each strategy fit together. When you can see the phases clearly, you can track the specific actions to achieve each phase.

Whenever you are going *from* somewhere *to* somewhere new, creating a visual roadmap is a helpful way to see, plan, and communicate what needs to be done as well as to share progress. When everyone sees where you are on a roadmap, it serves as a location and a next-steps tool for the team; it helps to remove ambiguity in a fast-moving situation and helps you make quick decisions.

This means you remain agile in the face of a short-term crisis and can take a necessary detour to achieving a vision if necessary. Adaptability and agility are key to ensuring strategy and action are always connected to the bigger picture and the needs of your consumer.

Having a strong management and operational skill set helps ensure that implementation happens in the most effective and efficient way to deliver results.

In a bigger organisation, you might have the luxury of an operations team that keeps the team on task. In a smaller organisation, where brand managers also drive the process, you might use workflow management software to automate or maintain a detailed view of implementation.

There can be tension between creative thinking and automated workflow. Remember that data and digital tools should always serve people. People don't go to work to serve automated workflow software – although if you're forced to use it, it can sometimes feel that way.

We are just at the beginning of our journey in developing digital tools to enhance human creative intelligence. They will continue to evolve so that they become seamless in their efforts to support us to achieve our potential.

With exhaustive brand and consumer data available, measuring the impact of your strategies is a lot easier than it used to be. As you build each strategy, you can establish defined KPIs (key performance indicators) that connect directly to the brand vision. This allows you to measure the progress of each strategy and, ultimately, to achieve your vision because you can clearly see the impact of specific actions or initiatives, based on the data. It's important to establish standardised KPIs so you can compare data over time.

QUESTIONS TO ASK WHEN DEVELOPING A STRATEGY TO ACHIEVE YOUR VISION

Insight

- Is your insight clear and in context? Do not continue to create a strategy until it is.

Problem

- Who exactly is the consumer you are solving a problem for?

- Have you articulated the problem to solve, clearly and in context?

Vision

- Is your vision for 'a world where. . .' clear?

- Will it position your brand to solve a particular problem?

- Does your vision articulate the *specific* shift you wish to create in the world?

- Can you demonstrate an authentic and definitive connection between your vision, your leadership messaging, and your intended impact internally and externally?

Mission

- Are you clear on your core competency and how you will use it to achieve your vision?

- Brands cannot solve every problem and be involved in every issue, so getting clear on the most important things for your company is critical.

Opportunity

- Is the business and brand opportunity clear?

Values

- Are your brand's values authentic and lived both internally and externally by everyone involved?

Strategy

- What are your broad areas of strategic focus that will deliver the vision?

- Strategic choices involve sorting through ambiguity and complexity. Have you elevated your perspective to consider the strategic whole before landing on your focus areas?

- Have you mapped the value that each strategy could deliver versus the ease of delivering it?

- Are your chosen strategies sharp and focused? Don't be afraid to say no to distractions.

- Does your strategy push the edges and take the brand, consumer, and world somewhere new and better?

- Are your key stakeholders clear on your priorities? Have your key stakeholders validated and resourced these strategies?

- Are you committed to delivering this strategy? Or, in your heart, are you developing this strategy only because it sounds like what you should do?

Planning

- How will you know when you've delivered each strategy?

- Do you have a prioritised and detailed action, process, resource, and measurement plan to deliver each strategy?

- What passions, strengths, skills do you need on your team? Rather than boxing talent into an org chart, can you take a more creative and empowering approach?

- Is everyone clear on their roles and responsibilities? Do you have a governance framework?

Action

- Do you have an operationalised roadmap over a specific time frame that will help to deliver efficiently and effectively?

- Action is as much functional as it is emotional. How are you involving, empowering, and inspiring your team?

COACHING QUESTIONS

Brands exist to benefit humanity, not the other way around. We need to make them work harder for us, and strategic clarity will allow that to happen.

The role of strategy is to align prioritisation of initiatives, resources, and action with the vision in a way that creates value in the future.

There is a difference between strategic thinking, strategic planning, and strategic implementation.

- Who are the best strategic thinkers in your organisation?

- Who are the best strategic planners in your organisation?

- Who are the best strategic implementers in your organisation?

- Do you have an aligned strategy and process from top to bottom and side to side?

Energy for strategic responsibility and alignment to create the future at the very top of the organisation is fundamental to transition a vision intentionally throughout the business. Without this energy and alignment, the organisation has an excuse to reject ownership of the vision or strategy to create a bold future.

- Hand on heart, are you committed, and is your leadership team energised and aligned with a clear strategy?

CHAPTER 8

LEADERSHIP

When I hear the words 'leader' or 'leadership', I imagine an original mindset. A bold perspective. An innovation that solves a real problem. A creative approach. A first mover. A courageous person who will stand up for what they believe in. A kind person. A person who believes in the potential of others.

In the corporate environment, the words leader and leadership have become ubiquitous. They mean so many things, for example: a collective term for the people leading the company, the act of leadership, the act of management, a manager, a leader of a team or project, a set of expected behaviours and processes, and the phrase 'everyone is a leader'.

No doubt my perspective reflects my values and experience. What's your perspective on the definition of leadership?

PERSONAL LEADERSHIP

Brands and the people who lead them can supercharge humanity's progress. Personal leadership is being clear about what *you* offer and understanding what you are willing to make a stand for.

Many of us spend a great deal of time in our professional lives following or leading other people. As a result, we can hopefully all remember a time when we experienced working with an outstanding leader.

One of the recurring themes that shone brightly during my

conversations with leaders in the research for this book is them recalling great leaders as being congruent, consistent, creative, connected, and compelling (the 5 Cs). *Congruence* above all else helps people trust in their leaders. Great leaders are remembered as being authentic individuals, having a powerful vision, and valuing other people's contributions.

What's your personal experience of a great leader? How did they make you feel? What were their values? What do you think motivated them?

As a leader of a big brand, everything that you and your teams create is a tangible reflection of you. You, your team, and your brand create a ripple effect in the world around you.

Your opportunity as a leader is to unlock creative potential in yourself and then others, your brand, and the world.

- What are your values?

- What motivates you?

- What do you believe in?

Creating time and space to answer these questions will inform who you are being as a human-first leader. There's no need to think like everyone else. Today is a new day and the beginning of the future. You have permission to unshackle yourself from the story that you've been telling yourself about who you are and how you should be. Trust your intuition, take a personal leadership position, and stand up for what you believe in.

- Have your answers to the questions above changed over time?

Through many coaching conversations with experienced C-suite leaders and tenured people on their leadership teams, many of them admitted they had reached a point in their career where they felt they had lost a big part of themselves and were questioning their purpose. Making more profit had lost its shine. Scaling for the sake of scale doesn't feel meaningful when you're one of the biggest brands in the world already.

By contrast, millennial leaders entering the C-suite in the 2020s believe that delivering on the new values of humanity is *the point* of their career. They wish to harness the collective intelligence of their teams to create a bold future for humanity.

They are often leaders of big teams, and empowering others to achieve their goals and dreams to create high impact fills them with joy. They understand they chart their own destiny to a better world by developing a sharp vision and a clear process. There is no doubt in their minds that they will create the impact they seek.

In leadership positions, this new generation will redirect the power of the biggest brands and immense resources at their disposal.

Their biggest challenges are convincing tenured Gen X leaders (those born between 1965 and 1981) and people without a vision for the future, that a clear purpose can be a powerful accelerator for profit and brand leadership.

- What's your purposeful vision?

As a leader with ultimate influence over the direction of a big brand, *you* hold the keys to your brand playing a role in creating a bold future for humanity and the planet.

You have the vision.

You have the brand.

You have the voice.

You have the resources.

You have the information.

You have the data.

You have the values.

You have the role.

You have the talent.

You have the valour.

If not you, then who?

PEOPLE LEADERSHIP

I believe that creativity is fundamental to what it means to be human. And being human-first is core to being a leader. The role of a leader is to lead the creation of, and then safeguard, the shared vision of the future, and to coach others to be their most brilliant selves whilst collectively working to achieve it.

Creativity comes in many guises within an organisation – creative thinking, ideation, innovation, strategy, problem solving, design, storytelling, and experiences are but a few examples.

As brands embark upon digital transformation initiatives in the 2020s, many are at risk of de-prioritising the value of creativity and human-first leadership. Remember, technology is simply a tool to enable human creativity.

Good people join good brands to do good work, but speaking from personal experience, once locked inside a big organisation and a particular type of culture, it's easy to get trapped in a mind-numbing vortex of politics and the push for efficiency gains, which can drain the originality and energy out of you.

As a leader, do you understand each person on your team and what strengths they bring? How can you help them remove the real and perceived barriers and unshackle their restraints to realise their potential?

I believe leaders should seek to uncover and celebrate unique strengths and boldness within their team because if you want your brand to make progress, you will need to harness maverick talent that can identify and push the edges. Often, people with these strengths are simultaneously held on a pedestal and vilified for thinking differently or provocatively.

I've noticed that thinking differently or being different can threaten some leaders when they, consciously or unconsciously, feel insecure about themselves or their position in a hierarchy. I'm not a psychologist but having experienced this phenomenon first-hand on several occasions, my intuition tells me it's a primal survival reaction to fear of losing control, or the potential to. A leader with high self-awareness and strong skills will recognise the dissonance and work through their bias towards this talented person and their strengths.

By asking powerful questions of the uniquely talented people around you, you can create an environment where all voices are valued. Your coaching can inspire creativity and change. Your role is to model an environment where people thrive.

It's not one voice in a team or the role of one leader that generates all the vision and all the trust necessary to create a bold future. Everyone must be able to show up with congruence and confidence so that the collective can thrive.

The best ideas come because of the trust that builds within the team through shared experiences, diversity of thought and experience, and because people feel inspired when they are part of something bigger than themselves and are growing.

In speaking to many leaders about the creative processes that teams move through, many of them reflected on their experience that spending time together as a cross-functional team also builds trust.

Leading an empowered cross-functional team as they work on creating a single-minded future for your brand is a dream scenario. In our conversations, leaders talked passionately of one empowered team creating one vision and strategy as being critical to their brand's success.

Cross-functional teams creating high-impact futures that include people from Innovation, Product, Design, Sustainability, Marketing, Strategy, Tech, Data, Legal, Operations, Finance, HR, PR, and Sales from global, geography, and local teams are typically energising and inspirational.

BRAND LEADERSHIP

Brand leadership can mean many things.

For example, some ways to measure brand leadership are to become the number one preferred brand in your key cities, or the number one brand by financial value, or the first to market with a particular innovation.

What about societal leadership?

Brands achieving visions of the future that reflect the values, ideologies, and interests of the people they serve.

Or innovation leadership?

Brands innovating solutions to enable humanity to make progress towards a better life, community, and world.

How does your brand measure its leadership position?

AN OPPORTUNITY FOR BRANDS TO CREATE A BOLD FUTURE

The events of the last few years have highlighted an opportunity for powerful brands to realise their full potential beyond commitments on their financial scorecard.

Established brands that have earned society's trust over time, and who have resources, talent, and influence at their disposal, are being asked by their consumers[28] to reinvest some of their extensive profits into creating a better future.

---

28 Based on my conversations with 18–22 year olds around the world between 2016 and 2019.

Brands with an eye on playing a role in proactively creating a purposeful future alongside their consumers are predicted by various reports[29] to be able to achieve an even stronger economic leadership position.

Brands have the influence to unite people and organisations who share similar values to create a shared vision for the future and then make that future a reality. But brands will not be the only entity with a powerful point of view and shared vision. They will also compete to shape the future alongside extremely powerful macro forces, for example geo-politics, data and technology, and social media.

Within this context, I believe there is an opportunity for brands to hold the highest intentions and to accelerate the potential of humanity. Their influential soft power has long shaped the culture, attitudes, and behaviour of those around the world to a great extent, and my experience inside some of the world's leading consumer brands informs me that there is an opportunity to do much more.

Of course, as Newton said, "For every action there is an equal and opposite reaction", and I can't help but consider the reality that, as with everything, there *may* be unforeseen consequences to brands playing an ever-increasing role in the future of society. To mitigate unforeseen consequences, responsible brands will engage in scenario planning to the very best of their abilities to make the right decisions about what sort of future they could create.

---

29 Including 2021 consumer products industry outlook: No-regret moves in the face of uncertainty by Deloitte.

As a global citizen who cares deeply about our collective future, I'd prefer to take a risk on accountable brands aligning with society to create a bold future than leave the creation of the future in the hands of powerful individuals with malevolent intent and ineffective governments that cannot get out of their own way, despite the pressing needs of humanity and the planet.

I believe brands are innately designed to lead with an informed point of view on the future and to innovate to solve problems for people and the planet in a way that helps us to create the life we envision.

COACHING QUESTIONS

Brands and the people who lead them can supercharge humanity's progress.

- What's *your* definition of leadership?

- How are you enabling your team to share their voices and strengths so they can play a role in creating our collective future?

- What's *your* role in supercharging progress and creating a bold future for our collective?

CHAPTER 9

LEADERSHIP VOICES

Let's hear from some leaders of brands who believe in supercharging progress and creating a bold future for humanity.

MELANIE STRONG

Partner at NEXT VENTŪRES Sports & Wellness VC

Melanie is an experienced Vice President with a history of leading diverse international teams and is passionate about serving communities that are unseen or unheard by mainstream business. Melanie believes that access to sports, the outdoors, education, and healthcare can transform culture. Following eighteen years at Nike, she is excited to build the next generation of sports, health, and wellness brands at NEXT VENTŪRES.

MELANIE

Having confidence in the power of your voice is so important. In this chapter of my career as an investor, I have learned how important it is for me and for the founders I partner with to use their voices. There's a sense of urgency because I want to see change happen in my lifetime. I don't think I had the same sense of urgency when I was younger, because I thought I was going to live forever. When I was younger, I also didn't *know* that my voice was valuable, but at forty-seven, I appreciate that my perspective is valuable because of my unique journey. I most enjoy using my voice to represent the unrepresented.

The pandemic created a *record-scratching* moment in terms of how we think about ourselves and our role in society, our community or our family, and the importance of connection and the power of supporting one another and thinking differently about our purpose. I've had a lot of conversations over the last year with people who now think differently about how they want to spend their time, whether because they faced a potential mortality crisis or because they hadn't seen their families in over a year. Sharing a common enemy has a way of creating clarity.

The pandemic was a common enemy that wasn't based on socioeconomic differences, gender, race, religious or geographic differences. The enemy was out of our control. I hope people have learned from the pandemic experience in terms of the power of an individual solving a problem versus the power of the *collective*. And I hope it can motivate us to tackle problems like climate change together. If we can attack things that can be culturally positive with the same fervour, I think we could see accelerated change.

What I wish for the future is that it would be based on kindness; people assuming positive intent, and expecting the best, not the worst. I think, as a culture, we're wired to assume the worst about ourselves and others. There is a self-fulfilling prophecy wrapped up in that mindset. When we expect the best from people, then I think we manifest people being their best.

I also wish for better access to healthcare and education, technology, and nature. I think about my disabled sister and how the world isn't available to her because of the barriers for someone with a physical disability. For so many, access to these fundamental benefits is still not available.

Through kindness and access, I believe society and culture can improve.

It's easy to confuse brands with organisations or technology. As an investor, I have a heavy bias towards investing in brands. Many founders are technical founders with a patent, or they've built a proprietary platform or technology, but technology isn't the brand; it's a functional service. Many founders are seeking funds to build a brand team and thus build emotion and meaningful connection with the consumer. There's such an interesting opportunity in this space because one thing we learned during all the crises of 2020, is that the companies in our portfolio who fared the best were the ones who had spent the time building a brand. Specifically, I mean brand marketing, not performance marketing. Those two things are often confused. Search Engine Optimisation (SEO) is not brand marketing. Brand marketing is about creating an identity based on a set of values through which you earn the right to serve your consumers, precisely because of your alignment with those values.

Younger founders build purposeful brands from the get-go. They don't have to play catch-up to make their brand values meaningful because they're building it in from the beginning. There's a great non-profit community called Kindred[30] for investors who care about using capitalism for good and using our existing social economic constructs to create a positive culture change. We focus on how we can create value metrics that we know are going to be important to this next generation of founders and consumers.

---

30 https://kindredmembers.com

Getting out there and spending time with young athletes or young founders who have a lot to teach investors like us about why they're inspired to create the companies is critical. I like to spend a lot of time with thought leaders and people who are thinking about the future – people who can see patterns and inform us about what's going to be different. The pandemic has created an interesting moment where some assumptions that we made around macrotrends that were informing our investment thesis may no longer be true going forward.

When companies have a powerful vision, it creates a tangible shift in the culture and the way leaders lead. A vision needs to play a bigger purpose than profit and growth. But today that's very hard because it's not valued by many shareholders and stakeholders. I think that's slowly changing, which is exciting, but whether you're a for-profit or venture-backed or a private company, non-profits do a much better job of sticking with the vision because they're held to a different expectation by stakeholders.

In the private sector, if you didn't start your company with a powerful vision of your contribution and build it into the structure and culture of the organisation, I don't think you could get there later because there are no incentives to do so. There's always going to be a desire to get bigger, to grow faster, and to scale. And so, if that's true, which I believe it is, then the incentive to do good for humanity and the planet must be foundational. It must be the way you onboard every employee. It must be built into your performance management and your performance reviews. It must be built into the culture and into every action in a truly credible way.

At NEXT VENTŪRES, one thing we do if we're onboarding our new teams is to do StrengthsFinder[31] together. In doing so, we've discovered that one thing we all have in common is self-assurance. We have an inner compass that gives us certainty in our decisions. I don't know where that comes from, but I think when you have self-assurance, it allows you to have confidence and belief in yourself that you can contribute to something bigger than yourself.

I will continue to use my voice and experience to create access to resources for founders who are doing work that I believe is going to help society be better. I want to be the fire starter who helps founders bring their brands to life.

TAMIKA ABAKA-WOOD

Creative + Strategic Thought Partner

Tamika is a Londoner currently based in Brooklyn. She aims to see things as they are now, then as they could be soon. Naturally anthropological and ethnographic, Tamika enables relevant brand strategy and impactful creative output.

Tamika has spent the past ten years developing and running people and community-centred research, insight, and foresight processes, and brand and innovation activations in 30+ cities across the world for clients such as Nike, Rimmel, NARS, Adidas, Clinique, Beats by Dre, Beautystack, and Converse.

She is also the co-founder and creative director of Plantain Papers, an annual print journal stocked at Moma PS1, Somerset

---

31 https://www.gallup.com/cliftonstrengths/en/strengthsfinder.aspx

House, and The Underground Museum. Tamika guest lectures on the University of the Arts creative practices course.

TAMIKA

Who decides who makes the decisions in society? Who decides who makes trends? Who decides who to listen to? We're in an interesting moment where everyone's got the potential to be heard. I think that using your voice to make sure that other voices are heard is so important.

We will never get out of our narrow way of thinking unless we invite other people into the conversation and listen deeply. The more we listen and cast the net wider to listen in a myriad of ways in a myriad of places, the better humanity will become.

Our attention has been hijacked by technology and social media, and by a short-term-profit cycle. In contrast, the question we should ask ourselves is, what does it take to be a good future ancestor?

What is good for communities right now might not be good in the next hundred, or thousand, or five thousand years. Of course, the impact is immeasurable for us because we are going to be long gone, but that doesn't give us an excuse not to try to do the right thing today, for people of the future.

I know I sound like a typical millennial, but the era of capitalism is tiny on the world's timeline. So, how do we commit to something bigger than ourselves? How do we get beyond the benefits of individual capitalism – beyond ego, titles, money, conspicuous consumption – so that we can be better future ancestors?

The future I envision is slower than the pace that the world works at right now. It's more thoughtful, more intimate, and it's connected. The future is exciting to me because the entire world is an unfinished blueprint and there's just so much opportunity to make it what we want. For example, today, we are living with the impact of what happened hundreds of years ago. We are experiencing the effects of the booming industry, which resulted in climate challenges. We have inherited an economic system and so many other systems that are not optimal. But what we have today isn't the way it's always been. Humans created those things, and it's important to understand that we can *uncreate* them.

Because we have foresight, we can create a better future. We must pay attention to those weak signals that show us what needs to be reconstructed to set us on the best course. Having the time and space to think about the future and to dream about transformation is a luxury. There are millions of people who can barely get by. We need to reshuffle the way our systems work because those people must be part of the conversation.

Many people have a very surface-level perception of what a brand is. I think about the Black Panther Party as an exquisite example of branding. An engaged and empowered society and culture have such potential to change how people think about themselves, what they think about others, and the world. Brands have got a huge opportunity to influence society and culture, but they are overwhelmed by an endless pursuit of monetisation.

Brands and Gen Z are equipped to co-create the future because of the wisdom passed down from previous generations. They are thought and creation partners in building a new world.

The good news is that behind many brands there are people who understand the real value and potential of a brand. And what they see doesn't satisfy them. They are audacious thinkers, who will dig deeper. They are hopeful and they believe in creating a better world.

The first step in creating a vision is unlearning: untethering yourself from the systems and the processes and the world that you've known for your entire life. It's important to be open to new insights. I know I'm onto something insightful when there's a sentiment or a feeling bubbling across industries that people can't quite grasp and struggle to articulate. It's a useful insight when it is bigger than me and my bias. We should think about what is timeless; human truths never go out of date.

We've been taught to keep our thinking small. We've been tricked into thinking that our role in the world is one-dimensional, static, and tiny, so creating a vision from that place can be scary. We haven't got a crystal ball, right? So, proposing a new vision feels dangerous, especially when it might exclude you from your community and there's not common language to communicate or understand it.

Nowadays, we can't predict where leadership will come from. In the past, most leaders came from the same schools and the same families. There is greater potential for leadership to come from anywhere. I think that's exciting. And I think leaders behind these brands need to recommit to who they are.

It's so easy to get caught up in the hierarchy of your job title and the materialistic proof that you *made it*, which is short-term thinking. But I believe leaders need to ask themselves what they are doing with their career and with their lives. What is their legacy? Leaders need to create the time to reconnect with who they are as human beings outside the ivory towers.

How about getting purposefully lost in what truly makes you come alive? Because then, you bring *that* sense of leadership to your brand and to our collective future.

SION PORTMAN

Chief Brand and Media Officer at Right To Dream

Sion is a Europe-based global brand leader. He believes that sport increases health, wealth, and happiness and is committed to encouraging people around the world to be more physically active by engaging teams to deliver innovative organisational and brand strategies focused on sports participation and development. Over the past twenty years, Sion has developed professional athletes, enabled global communities through digital and live experiences, and inspired millions through integrated marketing and content. Sion is also an English national governing body council member, volunteer, and mentor.

SION

Someone I greatly admire recently gave me a book – *The Second Mountain* by David Brooks. The book introduced me to a concept which has been valuable when I think about where I've been and where I'm going. David talks about a thin and a thick life. A thin life is what he calls *gold star winning*. For example, 'I got nine GCSEs, four A Levels, and my first job was in media. When I worked at Nike, I was promoted, and I did this great campaign and won an award.' Gold star winning is based on ego-driven achievement.

In contrast, he talks about the thick life. Who are you, what is your role within the broader community and how are you creating positive impact? I've experienced *some* elements of the thick life, for example volunteering or earning my football coaching badges so that I could help develop grass-roots sports. Another example was when we created the Football Academy at Nike to give an opportunity to kids who wouldn't normally be able to pursue a career in sport.

As the thick life has become increasingly important to me, the thin life has become much less so. In the last three years, I've become obsessed with sports participation amongst kids. Once you see the science and the statistics about who's playing, why they don't play, and the damage done when kids don't have the opportunity to play sport, the reality of what's happening hits home.

Did you know this generation of kids will be the first generation to die younger than their parents, largely because of their sedentary lifestyles? Once you see those stats, you can't ignore them, and it has driven me towards living a thick life.

Sport is so important to me because I moved around a lot when I was young, but everywhere I went, I could be part of a new group of friends within an hour by either going to the local pitch or joining the local rugby team. I just turned up, kicked the ball around, and gained ten friends, so it was my way of getting into the community. Kids don't have as much of that going on today. The digital playground is often what they find more fun, more sociable, and better designed for their needs.

As marketers, we spend a lot of time thinking about how we can get brands to be more purposeful and have a more positive impact. Global brands have a lot of money. They've got powerful voices. So, how can we redirect that influence from just selling products to also having a positive impact?

I recently did some research around sports participation in the UK. I've realised that it's the not-for-profit brands who operate like private sector brands that are doing the most interesting and impactful work because they were born out of making a positive impact. As marketers, maybe we should spend more time helping those organisations that *already* have a positive impact, to be stronger brands and develop a more powerful voice. I'll give you a couple of examples:

Football Beyond Borders[32] is a great organisation which is clear on its insight and impact. FBB impacts the lives of young people at risk of exclusion by providing them with skills and by helping them gain experiences to make a successful transition into adulthood.

---

32 https://www.footballbeyondborders.org/impact/

Forest Green Rovers is another example. A private company that positions themselves as the World's Greenest Football Club[33], they measure their success by their impact on society not just the result on the pitch. FGR is proving that sports clubs can lead the fight against climate change. For example, they are the only vegan football club and the first to be certified as carbon neutral by the United Nations.

Right to Dream[34] is a brilliant example of a not-for-dividend organisation built on a powerful notion that "everyone has the right to dream". Right to Dream gives youth the best chance of reaching their maximum potential and developing their character to the fullest. RTD is a football academy with exceptional performance *and* develops socially focused, highly educated purpose-driven leaders – not just footballers.

Using these examples, you can see that there's an opportunity for the world's biggest brands to take inspiration from the courage and authenticity of these brands. You can see the clear opportunity for stakeholders to measure success differently in order to insist that big brands play a more impactful role in society.

The reality is that right now, when you work in a big brand, you see they built the entire organisation for growth, not positive societal impact. Beyond consumer insights, marketing, environmental, social, and corporate governance (ESG) and impact teams, the overriding conversation is mostly about growth. Until CEOs and all stakeholders agree to a different way to measure success, I don't see how it will change. Will CEOs approach their boards and the stock market, and make the case

33 http://www.fgrfc.co.uk
34 https://www.righttodream.com/manifesto

that more growth will come if the brand focuses on doing the right thing?

Should we be repositioning brands to solve specific meaningful societal problems? Should we argue that it's better to measure participation statistics for kids in sport, or the health and happiness that results from kids doing sport versus only measuring financial metrics?

I see my role as a marketer as refocusing brands on a specific truth, solving meaningful problems, and creating momentum towards a better world. Brands should never be mediocre or play to the middle. They should always be bold and create change for the better.

NOTE TO
THE READER

THANK YOU

I'm so excited to share this book with you. Thank you for reading it. I believe that the future is ours to create and that leaders of powerful brands have the resources and voices to help create a better world. The tools I provide in this book have already delivered billions of dollars' worth of corporate growth, improved corporate cultures, and changed hundreds of lives for the better, so you can be confident they work.

BE BOLD

I absolutely believe it when I say that there's no need to think like everyone else. Today is a new day and the beginning of the future. You have permission to unshackle yourself from the story you've been telling yourself about who you are and how you should be. Trust your intuition, take a personal leadership position, and stand up for what you believe in. There is no one more capable or equipped to create a bold future than you.

NEXT STEPS

If you enjoyed *Brand New World*, I would be very grateful if you would consider leaving a review wherever you bought the book so other people can benefit from your opinion. Please recommend the book to others who you think would enjoy it so, together, we can create a bold future.

The content in this book is grounded in personal experience and learning, and insights derived from conversations with many CEOs, CMOs, brand and innovation leaders, and consumers around the world over many years. I've referenced sources to the best of my knowledge, but if you find a mistake, please let me know and I will certainly make the correction for the next edition of the book.

GET IN TOUCH

Are you ready to create a bold future? Many leaders don't have the time to get upstream to envision the future of the brand because the day-to-day reality of delivering results for the business and managing people is *intense*.

As a result, there's a high risk that strategic thinking doesn't happen, which gives the organisation an excuse to bask in inertia when it comes to creating a bold future.

Deep down, you know *nothing* can replace the knowledge and experience that you and your team have in envisioning the future of your brand, and you need help to:

1. Create time and space to get upstream

2. Get the right team of strategic thinkers in place

3. Unlock their vision for a bold future

4. Create an actionable strategy, brand positioning, and story

5. Connect with your own leadership philosophy and purpose

If you'd like more information about my work, to subscribe to my occasional newsletter, to download the bonus content or to get in touch, please visit my website: **www.createaboldfuture.com**.

ABOUT THE AUTHOR

Sarah J. Kay is the Founder of Create A Bold Future LLC, a global brand strategy consultancy.

Sarah is passionate about connecting with people and cultures first-hand to develop an informed perspective and a deep understanding of the problems to solve. She thrives on the challenge of taking brands into the future and unleashing creativity, talent, and passion in others to get there.

Originally from the UK, Sarah has twenty-five years of global brand, innovation, and leadership experience across multiple industries, brands including Nike, Reebok, and Mattel, geographies, categories, functions, and global moments such as the Olympics and the Football World Cup. She has lived in Portland, Oregon for eleven years.

Sarah specialises in developing transformative global brand strategy in collaboration with brand, innovation, design, product, and sustainability leaders. She takes a macro, forward-leaning approach to coaching to disrupt conventional wisdom in a positive way, to imagine possible new futures, and to synthesise complexity into tangible priorities and strategic clarity to inform decision-making.

Sarah has been an ICF certified professional coach (CPCC) since 2011. She empowers creators, innovators, and leaders to break paradigms about what's possible in the future.